WHAT DID YOU DO IN THE WAR, GRAM?

Roberta Olinger

CSN Books
San Diego, California 92119

What Did You Do In the War, Gram?
Copyright © 2012 by Roverta Olinger

ISBN: 978-1-59352-879-9

Published by:

CSN BOOKS
7287 Birchcreek Rd.
San Diego, CA 92119
Toll-free: 1-866-757-9953
www.csnbooks.com

Printed in the United States of America.

DEDICATION

This book was written at the request of my granddaughter Rachelle Monet Olinger and her interest in World War II. "How was it on the home front?" "What did you do?" The book also reveals the emotions of those searching for security without a Savior and trying to run away from problems.

ACKNOWLEDGMENTS

To Janet and Karen Hooper for their labor of love in preparing this manuscript.

To Patti and Mike Robinson for obtaining pictures and information from Boeing Aircraft Company.

To Lynn, Ron and David Olinger my computer helpers.

For the kindness and patience of Gary and Julie Kirk, CSN Books, to work with me through telephone and "snail mail".

I'm very grateful to all of you.

TABLE OF CONTENTS

DEDICATION iii

ACKNOWLEDGMENTS v

CHAPTER ONE 9

CHAPTER TWO 17

CHAPTER THREE 21

CHAPTER FOUR 29

CHAPTER FIVE 33

CHAPTER SIX 39

CHAPTER SEVEN 43

CHAPTER EIGHT 51

CHAPTER NINE 59

CHAPTER TEN 71

CHAPTER ELEVEN 79

CHAPTER ONE

The train chugged out of the station. As the wheels rotated faster and faster, I thought at last the train was putting distance between my troubles and me. Blue smoke crept through the coach that was filled to capacity with servicemen. Smoking was the custom of that day. The men were apprehensive and wanted to appear relaxed. Here I was on a troop transport train, not realizing that the priority was troops first – then civilian passengers, if room. But they had made room for plant workers joining the war effort, as in my case.

I had a window seat. I turned my head to escape the cigarette smoke of the two servicemen sitting beside me in a seat made for two people, not three. A trio of other men sat opposite us as we were at the front end of the coach. The "guys," not yet men, kept grinning at me accompanied by comments. The conductor came by and told them to "Straighten up. No more of that on this train." Perhaps he saw my plight so he came to my rescue. They heeded his warning making the trip better from then on.

Staring at the moving landscape, I thought back to 1938. How did all my dreams and plans vanish so quickly? My mother had died when I was five years old so in 1938 I moved from my grandparents' home in Redfield to Northville, South Dakota to keep house for my dad. I was not happy in the eighth grade; freshmen year was tolerable, but my sophomore year in Redfield was terrible. The drought in the thirties resulted in many losing their farms. Our farm, the Johnson homestead, was also lost, necessitating my being relocated.

The train whistle startled me back to reality. I looked ahead, but there was no town in sight. We were slowing down for a large intersection. How the engineer enjoyed blowing that lonesome whistle!

My dad had rented a house across the street from the school in Northville. There I experienced two glorious years of high school in my hometown with old friends. The former school had been more advanced, so I needed less study time. Even though I was very ill with scarlet fever before graduation, I managed to remain on the honor roll. A sidelight: My hair was thin after losing so much with the fever, but my girlfriend's sister, a beautician, set it in pin curls. When she combed and fluffed it out, it looked ample for the senior picture.

I had the lead in the Junior-Senior play, was editor of the school paper, and was voted queen of the first Jabberwalk (name for a fun day for the school and town), topped with the coronation. I yelled at basketball games, roller-skated, saw movies in the city of Aberdeen, cooked and cleaned for my dad and enjoyed friends. There were no computers or television that resulted in creative activities.

The war was on the horizon but it did not concern us, we thought. I started dating Harland Knudtson, a top student and farmer, who had serious thoughts of the future. Our class of 1940 scattered after graduation, some girls in college, the guys in the service, stationed – who knew where – as their locations were secret. There was no money for me to attend college, and Daddy thought I did not need it. I loved school so I felt left behind and lonely. Harland had left for agricultural college in Sioux Falls, South Dakota.

Harland and I had made marriage plans so I built on them. He had a farm with an attractive, but not large, house on it. The location was near his folks, not far from my home. The dreams I had for the future and my job kept me going.

"A date which will live in infamy," President Franklin Roosevelt announced, after hearing the news that Pearl Harbor had been attacked by Japan on December 7, 1941. Harland came home from college, joined the Air Force and went to boot camp in North Dakota. One winter day his father drove me to see him. His father and I got caught in a blizzard on the way home with no heater in the car. He covered me with a hairy skin robe. The snow beating against the windshield hindered our view. The car lugged slowly along until I rejoiced to see a dim outline of home. I pleaded with him to stay and thaw out but he left. They had no telephone and who would venture out in a blizzard? After several days of anxiety, I learned he had arrived safely.

Harland had a brief leave after completing his training so he came home. We were driving to Aberdeen for a day together.

"What would you like to have before I have to leave, a war bond or a diamond?" he teased.

I didn't answer.

"Well?"

I had hoped we were on our way to buy the ring.

"Open the glove compartment."

Not a very romantic proposal but when I took the ring box out, I experienced the thrill every girl feels when gazing upon a ring that promises so much. We were engaged!

He didn't want me to go to the train station when he left. It was a wise decision as I had shed enough tears the night before. No more roller-skating, hunting quail, catching fireflies at the pond – just work and waiting. Added to that was the thought of separation, worry at the late arrival of a letter and the big "if" he would return. All service mail had an APO address. His letters gave no clue to his whereabouts. He gave me his light brown sports jacket to make over for me. I sent him a picture modeling it when I finished remaking it.

The conductor came through the coach turning down the lights and checking on all of us. Sunset faded into darkness, squatting crapshooters left the aisle, and voices lowered to a murmur. All pointed to the day's end. I stood up to stretch and walk before trying to get a comfortable position to sleep. There were no sleeper cars on troop trains.

Sleep would not come to ease my thoughts. The black night hugged the window. Fear and loneliness took over; I was too far from home now. Things would be better from now on. I did cast an eye on the cord that ran over the window the length of the coach. One pull and the train would stop. Then what?

Memories continued to disturb my thoughts. Daddy and I left our happy home after Grandpa Johnson died. Grandma wanted to stay in their home in Redfield. Daddy and I left Northville to live with and care for her. I found employment at the Ration Board. My job at the Ration Board was in the

County Courthouse near the Highway Department where Daddy worked. I could ride with him or walk when it snowed during the night and partly buried the car.

When I had put in a day's work, my hand was glued to the pen, and I had a tired back and a cramped neck. Ration Boards were set up during the war to distribute goods needed to make planes, tanks, guns, bullets and bombs, and there were food stamps to insure that the troops were fed first. Gas and tires for cars were so limited that the farmers crowded the offices insisting that their needs were the greatest. They required fuel for tractors to plant the crops and tires for their pickups and cars. My job was to "smooth their feathers", fill out forms and put them on a spindle, explain when the limited supply would arrive and place their names on the bottom for notification. There was no guarantee how many tires or gallons of gas would be available for distribution. Some left in anger, others with worried looks. Growing up on a farm, I knew their desperate feelings. The farm's future depended on crops.

Grandma and Daddy seemed to argue about me so often that, weary of it all, I moved out. Great Aunt Sarah, Grandma's sister, and Uncle Pat lived in Huron, South Dakota. They had no children but were helping us "strays." I told Aunt Sarah about my misery. She helped me find a job in a drugstore there in Huron. I would live with them and work for my room and board. This I was happy to do. Uncle Pat, a railroad engineer, would be gone two or more days at a time. Aunt Sarah and I shared many laughs. The calm of her home gave me more peace of mind. She taught me her nightly routine that must be performed every night. She saw to it! "Always brush your teeth, wash your face, tip your head back to pat your chin twenty times with the back of your hands and then finish by reading the Bible." I was missing her already as I sat on the train.

The train screeched to a stop somewhere on the prairie. More soldiers boarded the already-full train. The kindly conductor shouted, "All aboard!" as the train resumed its journey with smoke from the engine adding to the darkness. My thoughts joined in.

In the exchange of letters with Harland, we decided to marry during his furlough.

"Oh wow! Aunt Sarah, good news!" I ran to her, Harland's precious letter in my grasp. We giggled and planned until his furlough. The girls at the Montgomery Ward store gave me a shower. I was second girl in the Department of Ladies' Dresses and would choose dresses that would go on the rack – ones suitable for sale in that area.

Harland returned and we had blood tests done. Then a day later he "dropped a bomb".

"I can't do it."

"What do you mean?"

"You do not know what it is like being a service wife. I can't take you into that situation."

No pleading would change his stubborn (wise) mind. When he left, I was back to square one: angry, humiliated, embarrassed and out of work because I had quit my job.

Uncle Pat had had his fill of all the tears and moping around. One night he said, "Why in *)*! don't you get out of this town? I just read in the paper that a man from Bocing Aircraft in Seattle is here looking for workers." Seattle? That seemed so far away.

"And they will pay your fare and train you. Your dad might be mad at me, but that sounds like a good deal."

It sounded better than anything I could come up with and I'd be far from my current situation. Arrangements were made. Someone wanted me. My spirits lifted and the trip became the focus – not what was awaiting me in Seattle.

I knew but one person there, Harland's sister Gladys. She thought he was a jerk for postponing the wedding. I wrote Gladys that I was coming as a recruit with my train ticket, room and training provided. She wired me back: "Don't come as a recruit. Stop. Pay your own way. Stop. You can stay with me one week."

I returned the ticket, packed my few belongings and with one hundred dollars cash, I boarded the train. So here I was – a complete flop, four years out of high school, on this crowded train heading for who knows what. I had never been out of South Dakota except once to Minneapolis, Minnesota to visit Gram Bechtel and Aunt Ceil. Aunt Ceil was studying art there.

After a fitful night's sleep, the soft light of dawn awakened me. My head was on a soldier's shoulder. He was still asleep so I moved slowly, as not to wake him, hoping he would never know. Quietly I stretched to get out the kinks. It wasn't long before the murmurs and groanings became louder as everyone looked out on the day that would take us into different futures.

Getting my body upright, adjusting to the movement of the train, I started down the aisle. What a relief! I could walk. A buzz went through that we were nearing Seattle. The prairie was replaced with trees, mountains, more homes, followed by the city.

"Seattle is the next stop. Gather your belongings," the conductor announced.

CHAPTER TWO

I was fascinated by it all. The thought never occurred to me – what if Gladys wasn't there to meet me? The engine brakes ground to a stop, the engine let off a cloud of steam and the doors opened. So many faces but I spotted faithful Gladys among them. The greeting was brief, followed by, "No time to lose! Places are scarce so we have to start looking."

She continued talking but I heard very little of what she was saying. There was so much to see: tall buildings, stores, people and more people. Seattle had become a "boom town" with Boeing employees, servicemen being shipped in and out and whatever else is needed during wartime.

We boarded what looked like a big bus. A long pole on top connected the trolley to a wire that supplied power for a smooth ride. One put little green plastic tokens into a glass "box" which was placed on the end of an iron stand. Gladys was telling me about the life of a Boeing recruit: You would be put in a room with others – not in a desirable area – transportation problems...I brushed it aside by thanking her for helping me.

I freshened up, ate a bite, and tried to walk off the movement of the train. Gladys lived several flights up.

"How come there is no screen on the window?"

"There aren't any flies here." Oh, I thought I must be in heaven! In Dakota we fight off flies until the snow falls.

"We just have a week to get you settled. ONE WEEK, my landlady informed me, so let's go."

Gladys had the "Rooms for Rent" section of the newspaper firmly in hand. An afternoon of searching produced no rooms available. It didn't concern me too much as all I wanted was to sleep in a bed that night.

Gladys worked for Boeing Aircraft. She asked everyone she knew where she could find a room, put "Room Wanted" requests up in her work area, and scanned the paper daily – nothing. If anyone could find a room, it was Gladys who was a "real go-getter". At the end of the week her landlady said that I had to leave. I didn't have much money, but I was sort of numb by that time and lost in the wonder of my new city.

The last day Gladys came home with a faint hope. Someone had told so and so, so and so had told what's-her-name, and finally it got to Gladys that a lady was taking over a fraternity house in the university district. So many young men had been drafted or left for the armed forces that the houses were rented to accommodate the influx of workers. No men were left there, of course.

It was dark and raining lightly as we walked from the bus to an address on "Frat Row". A lady was struggling to carry a rolled up carpet in the front door.

"Must be the place," Gladys assumed.

When she inquired, the lady asked, "How did you know I would have a room to rent? I haven't advertised nor am I moved in."

"Rumors, good ol' rumors. My friend needs a room desperately," Gladys stated.

"My name is Alta Crossen. I'll need rent in advance. You're on your own for breakfast. You can fix a lunch and I'll serve dinner."

I didn't have enough money for the rent. She looked me up and down as Gladys pleaded. She was assured I had a job at Boeing, had nowhere to stay plus all the other pitiful things Gladys could conjure up. Alta relented. What a sigh of relief! But, now we needed to get Gladys' landlady to let me stay until my room was ready. The final hurdle cleared and we fell exhausted into bed.

The "Boeing Girls" at the boarding house.

Landlady, Alta, center with her mother and the
"Boeing Girls" at the boarding house.

CHAPTER THREE

After that, my life took a complete turn from a farm girl to a small town girl in her early twenties, to a big city gal. Some adventures have faded from memory: how I found a ride to and from work with Waldo who taught me to read the blueprints for the beautiful B-29 bomber, time frames and other details. But I DO remember my first room. The address of the fraternity house was 4714 17th Ave. N.E., Seattle, Washington.

There were three floors of rooms. Mine was on the second floor. It had bunk beds (I'd never slept in a bunk bed), a table, a chair and a lamp where I spent off hours writing to Daddy and Harland. Some evenings the rain sliding down the window brought on homesickness, but by morning my new world erased it from my mind.

About a week later Alta greeted me with, to her, exciting news: "I found the perfect roommate for you! She'll be moving in tomorrow." Adeline from North Dakota would be a stranger sharing MY room. Selfishly I thought, "Well, I'm not going to sleep in the top bunk." I'd bumped my head enough times getting used to the lower. I couldn't see myself climbing up and down. My guard was all built up when I came home from work. She was nice and friendly, didn't mind the upper bunk at all and was happy to be there to help the war effort. I sheepishly shrunk to a foot tall. She was on a different shift, so she came home before me. She would take down my laundry, fold it and place it at the foot of my bunk many times. We went places together and kept in touch until the day she died.

Waldo, in his late thirties or early forties, was "Old Faithful", always arriving on time with a car full of Boeing workers. How he found the plant in that dense fog some mornings was a marvel – I could not see a thing.

I don't recall ever being late. We had to clock in on time cards so, if late, our pay would be docked (taken from our paycheck). Five minutes late meant docked for fifteen minutes. Docking went by the quarter hour. Waldo eagerly waited to hear the stories from the night before. We told him about our dates, where we went and news from home. He rejoiced with us or sympathized when we had bad experiences. He was just a dad figure with a big shoulder.

Blueprint classes ended much too soon. It was exciting to learn what made planes fly and why certain parts were needed. I fell in love with airplanes and flying. Blueprints were similar to figuring out a dress pattern and fitting all the pieces together. Gram B. had taught me well on that. But, par for the government, they took me to a warehouse where materials were received and stored until used. I was an office girl! I was the only girl in the office.

The work was boring and slow, just checking and stamping receiving orders. When someone was coming to the warehouse, my boss would tell me to hold back the orders and stamp them while he was there. To pass the time I wrote letters and drew pictures, feeling guilty taking a paycheck. I learned about government waste. The boss was a young punk playing "big shot". One day a man came and asked how I liked my job so I told him that there was not enough work to have a secretary. In a couple of days a transfer came through. My boss was furious, read me the "riot act" but I was too happy to care. I thought they would transfer me to blueprints for which I'd been trained. I had reminded the man of my training and my desire.

Think again. My new position was a step up in the office to Plant #3. That turned out to be great. Not that I liked office work any better, but my boss and fellow employees were tops. Waldo continued to be a faithful driver. He worked for the Continental Can Company that had been converted to making plane parts during the war. The location was near Plant #3. He dropped me off, pointed at the entrance and drove off. I had never seen such a huge building. People were swarming in and out like bees. I followed the 'bees' but just stood, once inside the door. Where do I go? I managed to find a person who gave me a time card, showed me where to clock in, led me to a large rectangular office with a number of windows to introduce me to Ray Sowers, my new boss. He was a kindly, farm-type man, ample dark hair with a slight wave, sturdy build, but best of all, a welcome smile. I missed my dad and relatives who were my security, but Mr. Sowers radiated that type of protection. As time went on, he proved he cared for the employees in his department, Receiving Inspection.

People came in and out of the office. Mr. Sowers was in the construction area a good deal of the time. He was keeping a watchful eye on and befriending the workers under him. A blue button was pinned on my blouse. This button allowed me the freedom to go into all areas of the plant until the termination of my job. Workers were confined to the area in which they worked. One of my duties was to go to different areas to pick up or take communications. In addition, I inspected extrusions, which were long pieces of metal, after another worker had finished measuring them. Everything was carefully checked with back-ups.

One inspector was careless. I noted several errors almost weekly. Forms with the corrections were taken to the office. One day he was reading a comic book while sitting on a pile of extrusions. I was furious – more government waste. I had never seen someone "putting in his time" by not being productive. In my world, he would have been run off the farm in haste! The work ethic that I was taught was "to do your best at every job and EARN your pay." Grandpa informed us from the Bible, "If anyone will not work, neither shall he eat" (2 Thessalonians 3:10). I liked to eat. This inspector got away with his slackness. In fact, he delighted in it. His hourly wage was more than mine, yet I had to correct his work! The lives of pilots and test pilots depended on our accuracy in all the building stages.

There were other office tasks, but I hurried to complete them so I could wander through the work areas. That blue button gave me an education in all the steps that went into the construction of the beautiful B-29 bomber. One area had all rivet inspectors. There were different sizes and colors of rivets. Elizabeth Gambs sat on a high stool before a tall square desk on which were boxes of them. She had a tiny metal ruler to measure rivets in each box. If there were any that were not up to the standard length or width for that size, the entire box was discarded. She would reach in a box on the floor by her stool and take out another pile of boxed rivets when she completed the boxes on her desk. That to me was the most difficult job in the plant. Some of the rivets were so tiny. She never complained. I saw her every day when picking up papers from that station.

We had two fifteen-minute breaks: one in the morning and the other in the afternoon with time for lunch. But it was still a long time for Elizabeth to perch and measure hour after hour. She and I became good friends. She was an older, stocky in build, single schoolteacher from North Dakota. We ate lunch together sitting on the long, large wooden dock when weather permitted. We would open our lunch boxes after dangling our legs over the side. We shared many things such as what city and state we had left, our dreams and our present situation.

One time she took me to her aunt's home on Hood Canal. What an experience! We went in a rowboat to collect oysters for dinner that evening. Berry bushes hung along the shore where the ground was higher. We picked and ate as we glided along, her aunt rowing. When we had enough oysters, we went back to shell them. I was not too fond of that but tried my best with the slimy creatures. Her aunt would drop them into a pot of boiling water. It was enlightening to see the process of preparation. The oysters we had at home had been in jars. Her home was sitting all cozily in among the beautiful evergreens. She was such a delightful hostess! I was reluctant when it was time to depart. Reality soon took over as the ferry docked in Seattle.

There was one black lady who sat with us for lunch. She was so pleasant and friendly that we would walk and talk as we returned to our areas. We had no contact out of the plant, however.

Clock-in time for me was 7 a.m. sharp or before. During the afternoon break, I would lie down to rest when my previous night's activities had been tiring. There was always someone to wake me if I fell asleep, but the benches in the women's restroom were not that comfortable. Many times I put my hair in pin curls that I brought to work. We were required to wear a scarf at all times. I covered the pins during the day so that my hair was curled when I went out in the evening.

We Can Do It!, *created in 1942 for Westinghouse by Pittsburgh artist J. Howard Miller.*

The daily routine never became boring as some office jobs; "Rosie the Riveter" became representative of female workers. As the metal pieces were fit together, "Rosie" and the men climbed over that section of the B-29 until it was completed and the next one came on the assembly line. There were welders with shielded eyes and blue-flamed torches in another area. I didn't look too closely at that process. Windshields installed, instruments put in the cockpits, seats, so many details plus multiple inspections, but the joy of seeing that silver bird roll out of the hanger was awesome. The many who saw only rivets, only extrusions, only a small part, could now see the results of working together. That B-29 would be used to defend our country, our way of life and eventually would drop the atomic bomb.

A city with fake buildings, trees and shrubs was built on the roof of the Boeing plant. Hopefully the plant would not be sighted from the air. There were air raid drills to evacuate the building just in case. That was no small job with so many employees. One day all power went out, the siren gave warning and out we scrambled. I had just purchased a good pen. I ran back to save it. It was the only thing of value I had at work. A stern reprimand reminded me that if it had been a real attack – dumb, dumb! As it turned out, the blackout was not caused by anything serious. Everyone returned soon after the scare.

CHAPTER FOUR

Gladys was busy with her life. She would give me news of Harland, if any. I no longer lived from letter to letter but never stopped believing that we would make up after the war was over. At one point I took a night job so I'd be too exhausted to lay awake and cry. That job lasted maybe two weeks. My energy was giving out plus the office was in an undesirable part of Seattle. The men working there would be charged with harassment today.

The USO was looking for hostesses. It was similar to the canteen in Hollywood that was famous with all the stars working there. In Seattle one did not serve food but gave little services such as notepaper, pens, stamps, conversation and dancing, all available to those in the service. After an interview, I was given a USO ID card with my picture and address on it. This was to be worn all the time I was in the building. The music and dancing plus all the activities were on the main floor. My job was – you guessed it – in the office upstairs.

A good part of one evening was taken by a young man relating all the wonderful things about his girl back home.

He told me about the good times they had had and the places they went together – everything I was trying to forget. He completed the letter to her to which I attached a stamp and deposited in the "outgoing" box. We talked a bit more then he left. Pity and anger followed me home that night.

My lady boss dashed into the office a few evenings later.

"Do you dance?"

"Yes!"

"Go downstairs quick. We are short of hostesses tonight."

The rules were that you did not turn down anyone who asked you to dance, did not become overly friendly and absolutely did no dating or it was "curtains".

Ordinarily I loved to dance. Gram Bechtel told me Grandpa danced the polka with me before I could walk. He would sweep me up in his arms and away we'd go, much to my glee. That night at the USO it was a chore. I performed my assignment so well that I did not work in the office again. I danced with guys from the east to the west coasts, north and south, and from Texas. The latter were still on a bucking bronco, I thought. There was jitterbug, waltz and the two-step to which we twirled and swirled, on or off beat – it didn't matter. Some evenings my arms felt as if they would fall from the sockets. BUT...I did not have trouble falling asleep.

The USO and YMCA sponsored interesting trips for the men in uniform. I don't recall what was available for the women. Girls were chosen to be partners for the guys during the outing. My first event was lunch and a day spent on a yacht. I returned to the dock with a red face, which they told me, was not sunburn but wind burn. The day was so much fun and something I had never done before in my life.

There was a ski trip planned that would take us to beautiful Mt. Rainier. Skiing was foreign to me but I had seen pictures. Hank was one of my partners from the USO. He encouraged me to sign up for this trip; this was not a date but my job, we reasoned. He was a good dancer with a pleasant personality. Two of my girlfriends had also volunteered, so it would be a fun time.

The day came for our outing. We got on the bus that was about to pull out when Hank came running up. I heaved a sigh of relief as he got on board. All of us settled down for a most enjoyable trip; the scenery was breathtaking, postcard perfect, with snow-laden evergreens emitting a fragrant pine perfume.

When the bus stopped at the ski lift, we scrambled to rent our equipment. None of us had ever been here, but we didn't look for direction signs. We simply followed the people to a rope lift. Ropes were going up and coming down. Skiers just grabbed the rope and glided up the mountain. The difficulty, I learned, was that balance was necessary at all times. Under the rope I went and found myself going back down between the ropes. People were going up and those coming down stared in disbelief. A motor operating the lift loomed in front of me. I had no clue how to stop. I sat down and turned sideways just in time. Hank came to the rescue but I didn't appreciate his laughter. We learned later there was a beginner's slope plus an area to practice what one should know before skiing – stopping was one of the necessary skills.

Pictures were a must. So after removing the skis and having hot chocolate at the lodge, we walked up a path to a quiet scenic area. What could be a better background than the trees whose branches were weighted down with pure white, wet snow. Friend Linda was a "camera bug" so she positioned us on the path. She wanted two on the path with the other two beside them. The legs of the two off the path disappeared in the snow as it was so soft and fluffy. Linda and I were from South Dakota where winds pack dry snow so hard that you can walk on it. It was good for a laugh. We went to the lodge to dry off before the trip back. I had to write home about that outing!

Friends

CHAPTER FIVE

America was changing. Little flags with blue stars appeared in more home windows. Each star represented a person who was in the service from that family. My classmates and cousins of acceptable age were drafted or joined up, health permitting. More women and young girls out of high school were leaving home to work in plants or factories. My Aunt Irene went to Wisconsin where she made parts for bombs. The small towns grew smaller with the exodus. Farmers and some of their sons were exempt from the service because food was essential, especially for the troops. Those who had a 4F rating for other than physical reasons were held in low esteem, as were those who went to Canada to escape the draft. Those with a 4F rating did not participate in the armed forces.

Slogans on posters were everywhere in the United States, such as "Zip your lip or sink a ship". Rosie the Riveter was on posters with the words, "We can do it!" She was pictured rolling up the sleeve of her blue denim work shirt to reveal substantial muscle. Her ID button was pinned to her collar and her hair was neatly tied in a red and white polka dot bandanna. She was an attractive but serious young woman. Other war slogans were: "Shut my mouth for Uncle Sam" and "Achoo in the Fuehrer's face". "Buy Bonds" posters were seen everywhere. All the movie theaters promoted the sale of war bonds.

Illustrator James Montgomery Flagg designed the recruiting poster with the famous image of Uncle Sam.

The most prominent poster was "Uncle Sam Wants YOU!" His pointed finger and serious gaze looked right into your soul, no matter the viewing angle. Young men left the farms and cities to volunteer before being drafted. Spirited band music and cheering crowds sent them off as they boarded the trains, but the cheering was soon replaced by tears, longing looks, prayers and fears that the soldiers would never return. They watched as the chugging loco-motives pulled the coaches carrying their loved ones to an unknown destination. The only address would be an APO that would afford no clue. The soldiers' letters forbid them to mention or give a hint as to their location. Correspondence was censured in some cases. When mail home was delayed, fear set in: Missing in action, wounded, prisoner or killed in action could be the next news.

On July 13, 2006 a report on the radio stated that a WWII plane and the remains of the pilot downed in some remote area were found by wild animal hunters. Sixty-one years later, the soldier's family had an answer.

Bob Hope, a popular entertainer during the war, continued to take Hollywood stars to entertain and cheer up troops in various locations. Many times they were dangerously close to the front. The servicemen and women enjoyed every moment: laughing, whistling, clapping and even shedding tears, especially when "White Christmas" was sung. The performers brought a bit of home to the men.

Rain, mud, uncomfortable living quarters, quite the opposite of their splendid homes, were endured. Jeeps replaced Cadillacs, field rations for expensive dinners. The troops were subject to sudden evacuations in case enemy planes came too close, but we did not hear one complaint. Frances Langford, Rosemary Clooney, Red Skelton and others made many trips. A number of pretty girls adorned the stage also. Bob always had jokes about the location, camp food, officer or anything that pertained to their situation.

Rationing was tightened as the fighting intensified. Drives sought for every usable piece of metal. Toothpaste was sold in metal tubes. People were urged to trade in empty tubes when purchasing another one.

Ladies took special care of their nylon hose as they had to last. This applied to the women in the service also. Nylon was used for parachutes, for one thing, and couldn't be manufactured fast enough. Paratroopers were shot down like sitting ducks during invasions. They suffered broken ankles and legs or were captured before they could bury their chutes and escape.

As for the patriotic side of this war, everyone in the states was affected by the conflict whether or not he or she had family members in the service. Americans, as a whole, were united – doing all they could to support the war effort to halt Hitler and Mussolini as well as the Japanese.

Children collected scrap metal, pieces of foil, old aluminum pans, tin cans, newspapers, wire, fat and cooking grease. They would pull their red wagons going door-to-door plus combing streets and alleys.

Piggy banks were emptied to buy victory bonds and we also collected Blue Chip Stamps which allowed us to purchase different household products. Some schools taught knitting to sixth graders on up. They knitted scarves and squares that were sewn together for afghans.

Adults planted victory gardens if they had a plot of ground, large or small. Food was a priority for the troops. The garden food was for the families.

People donated blood. Celebrities were shown donating to encourage others to do likewise. Blood drives were held often.

Women knit socks, sweaters, scarves and lap robes. They wrote letters, rolled bandages, and helped the Red Cross in whatever way they could. Jobs vacated by men leaving for the service were filled by women. Young women in their twenties and older, and even some housewives entered plants that built ships, planes, made ammunition or some other material used for the war.

Women and teenage girls served coffee, sandwiches and doughnuts at railroad stations when troop trains made brief stops. The men would hang out the windows as the ladies walked alongside handing out the treats. The women held the families together through it all.

National unity to protect our loved ones, our freedom and our country was the goal. General Eisenhower said, "Hitler should be aware of the fury of an aroused democracy. We are all in this together." If someone complained of a shortage, they heard. "Don't you know that there is a war out there?"

War bond drives were held by Hollywood stars. Part of my salary went toward one bond that I kept. It came in handy after I was married. Ration books were issued like the ones for gas and tires. This put a limit on the purchase of sugar, meat and other items needed for our troops. Banana boats were used to transport goods to the military. I longed for a banana before the war ended.

Nylon hose were as scarce as hen's teeth. If one of us girls was fortunate enough to date a serviceman who had access to a pair now and then, she was envied. Chocolate bars were another treat for the guys and were a priority for service personnel. Cigarettes were not in short supply. Cartons of them managed to be delivered to even the most out-of-the-way places. It was the same with Spam, a canned meat that had a "reputation" and afforded many jokes. It was the main staple according to reports.

Some results of the civilian efforts were reported by President Roosevelt: in four years the United States increased airplane production from 40,000 to 50,000 per year then to 96,380 per year. The army had over eight million fighting men, the navy had four million, and the Marine Corps had one-half million men. The United States had the best equipped service personnel in the world. All this, added to the forces of England, France and other allies, makes it difficult to comprehend the immensity of the invasion of D-Day.

CHAPTER SIX

Back at the office, after picking up the mail and filling out the inspector reports, I would sort them and then deposit them on Mr. Sower's desk. Outside the long row of windows on the north side of the room, one could view a large empty field. It did not stand empty for long. Damaged planes were lined up for repair, making the reality of war quite evident. I wondered as I saw them, "How did they fly in that condition?" Machine gun bullets gorged the wings, had damaged the motors, had bent the propellers, and cockpits were peppered with holes. How badly were the pilots wounded? Amazingly, they had brought the planes down safely. Small painted Japanese flags adorned the fuselages to indicate the number of enemy aircraft shot out of the sky by the pilots and crews. The aircraft that could be repaired were returned to combat.

Every plane, ship, tank and jeep was needed as the losses were innumerable. Equipment loss could not be compared to the loss of lives, however. Thousands of men died in one day's battle. I chose not to think about it.

The people in Europe were suffering from bombings, the invasion of German troops, fires amidst crumbled buildings and hours spent in bomb shelters.

Then there was the Holocaust of the Jews. When it was revealed to the world after the war was over, it was unbelievable to people here in the United States. The Holocaust remains a shadow of man's cruelty to man. European Jews were forced to wear armbands that set them apart from other citizens. They were taken from their homes day or night. The able ones were sent to work in factories making weapons for the German troops or wherever they could serve the war effort.

Two hundred fifty calories of German food was their daily allowance. Old men, women and children loaded in box cars, crowded like cattle, cold and without sanitary facilities to dispose of waste, were shipped to concentration camps or to gas chambers. Those who survived the trip were eventually killed in the gas chambers. Their bodies were burned or dumped in ditches making it impossible for families to find loved ones or to find out what had happened to them. Those in the camps died of starvation or disease. After the war the German people admitted that they had known but had turned their backs. Hitler was making a super race.

There were a few survivors who told their stories and began life anew. Years later I heard Corrie ten Boom from Holland relate conditions there plus the fate of her family (I highly recommend her book, *The Hiding Place*.). Her whole family was caught hiding Jews and both families were taken away. She and her sister, Betsy, ended up in a concentration camp. The book gives vivid descriptions of the hard life, God's provision for her and Betsy, plus her release at the end of the war. Thereafter, she traveled many miles to a number of cities telling her story, even though she was getting up in years.

CHAPTER SEVEN

To offset all this destruction and madness, there was beautiful Seattle. There was the wonder of roses in December, gorgeous rhododendron bushes heavy with blossoms and an abundance of green trees year 'round. It was a very restful scene. The clear blue water of Lake Washington was adorned with graceful sailboats and ferries navigating back and forth to the islands, with the Bremerton ferry being extra crowded with service personnel. All these things were new to me.

The list continues: Greenlake was not frozen in winter but enfolded in a green grass carpet with trees and colorful flowers; bicycles for rent resulted in happy cyclers circling the lake. The beaches of Lake Washington were dotted with tiny red fires at night that scented the air with burning wood. And Puget Sound was enormous. I'd never seen so much water! South Dakota was relatively flat except for the Black Hills. The majestic range of Olympian mountains with snow covered peaks pure white against the blue sky were a wonder. Then there was Mt. Rainier crowned with snow that could be seen from Seattle, depending on the weather of course. I wrote Daddy every week, but there wasn't enough paper and ink to describe it all!

People from all over the United States and Canada were involved in "the effort," working together for victory with the assurance we would win. "Freedom is not free" but Uncle Sam, pointing his finger at us from his poster, made us feel, "He wants me."

Much entertainment was available. Not only the magic of the Crystal Ballroom, but the concerts of top bands. Duke Ellington in person was one of my favorites. Gene Krupa excelled on the drums, but the music would stop while he went into his frenzy. Usually the solo was so long that we had to stop dancing and stand until he finished.

One time a few of us girls decided to be brave and go to the Gypsy Rose Lee show. We thought we could leave if it got too risqué. Gypsy was the stripper at that time. She and her girls were discreet, nothing like what one would expect. I was relieved as I was brought up to believe that that kind of behavior was a big no-no, and I felt very sinful going along with the gang. In later years, television programs and commercials had more nudity, which were taken as the norm.

Continuing on the lighter side, there were more adventures living with a group of Boeing girls and Seattle teeming with servicemen from all branches of the services. Oh, so many things to do and see – never a dull moment. We managed to wash our hair and clothes, take bubble baths, and eat dinner. Alta served delicious food. Sometimes one of us had a dinner date. The number around the table varied but she didn't mind. Alta always enjoyed being a part of our lives.

The large living room had heavily draped windows, sofas, chairs, tables and a Victrola phonograph afforded many happy evenings when the guys came to visit. But, everyone had to vacate that room by midnight.

Every evening could be party night with the abundance of entertainment that was available. All-night movies, dances, concerts, celebrities visiting clubs, big bands coming and going were how we spent a few of the great nights in Seattle.

Ships were docking. Ships were leaving. Troop trains pulled in to drop off their passengers. Soldiers, sailors, Air Force personnel, Seabees, and members of the Coast Guard filled the city. Coming from a small quiet town in South Dakota, I felt as if a whirlwind were sweeping across the prairie. The electric busses and taxis never lacked passengers.

The following is a list of special memories taken from my diary:

- First ski trip
- First dance on the U.S.S. Yorktown Carrier (a guest of a sailor who requested a partner from the USO)
- Saw Gypsy Rose Lee and girls
- Attended the International Regatta
- Went to a Duke Ellington concert
- Saw Bob Hope and his show
- Heard and saw the Andrew Sisters
- Listened to the Ink Spots in person
- Took a trip to the ocean, Copalis Beach
- Attended my first and last frat dance. Wilmac Whistler was my partner. Acacia was the name of the frat house.

- Was a bridesmaid in Aunt Irene's wedding
- On December 11, 1946 I left for Los Angeles.
- Arrived in Los Angeles at 7 p.m. on December 13th in pouring rain.

The dance on the carrier has a special memory, although it was not pleasant at the time. I had met a sailor when his mom came to Seattle to visit him and she contacted me. She was a friend of my grandmother. Mother Maude, a cousin and I had dinner with the sailor. Denny was on the Yorktown the day I was there. He saw me walk in with my partner who was assigned to me for the day. Denny called out to us, so we went over to where he was standing. He outranked my partner and made it apparent by insisting I come with him to see the purser's headquarters, his job. We obliged but not willingly. (That purser became my husband.) I apologized to the sailor, but that episode spoiled the tone of the day.

A date with "just another serviceman",
Navy Purser, Denny Olinger—
who became my future husband.

It was educational to tour the carrier, to see the short space where planes landed, and to see the elevators bringing planes up and lowering them again. It was a festive time with family and friends of the crew enjoying time together, but the piping of officers aboard was a bit piercing to the ears.

The carrier was docked in Portland, Oregon, so I had to take a return flight to Seattle. It began to rain – more like pour. The flight was delayed. This was Sunday evening and I had to be at work early Monday morning. Midnight came and went but finally we took off, and I did make it just in time for work. It was difficult to keep my eyes open that day.

Duke Ellington was truly a "Duke". Irene and I attended his concert. His music kept my body in motion but Irene sat so still. How could she? His band was excellent, so full of rhythm.

The Ink Spots' voices blended together in exceptional harmony. They created a more mellow mood, soft and more relaxing. I purchased several of their records. It was a pleasure to limber up or relax to music rendered by both instrumental and vocal groups.

Sundays at Alta's allowed time for talking, odd jobs or going someplace together. Portable record players were popular. Records called platters were in abundance so we chose our favorite vocalist or band, packed up and headed for Greenlake. Once there, we cranked up the player, put on a platter and then danced on the grass. If we had the money, we would rent bikes and ride around the lake. The green grass, blue water and the sky with fluffy white clouds floating above us made for a perfect relaxing afternoon. Many people were there, yet the area did not feel crowded.

Harland's unit was in Seattle for a short time. When he called and came out to see me, one of the girl's dates that day had a car. Several of us piled in with our sandwiches and pop (soft drinks) and drove to the river. The bottles of pop were secured among the rocks in the river while we explored the area. Ferns grew under the trees. The pines perfumed the air with their fresh fragrance. Some of us chose stones that caught our eye; the water was so clear that we could see them all along the water's edge. How smooth they were with years of constant water flowing over them!

Our appetites told us it was time for sandwiches so we returned to rescue the pop from its watery prison. It had not "escaped" but was ice cold – cold as the river water. We sat on blankets spread on the riverbank and devoured the lunch before us. Harland seemed to enjoy everyone. I so hoped this would be the day that we made up. But it was not the day nor would that day ever come.

The forties brought forth numerous songs. "Big bands", small or famous, toured the country plus going overseas to entertain our servicemen. Radio was in its heyday, reaching the troops to build morale. Tokyo Rose, a young lady from Japan, was on the radio trying to tell the allies they were losing the war. She didn't succeed but became the object of many jokes.

A few hit songs were:

"I'll Be Seeing You" – Tommy Dorsey

"There'll Be Bluebirds over the White Cliffs of Dover" – Jimmy Dorsey – (The Dorsey brothers had top bands)

"In the Mood"

"Don't Get Around Much Anymore" – Duke Ellington"

"Tie A Yellow Ribbon Round the Old Oak Tree"

"It Had To Be You"

"When the Lights Go on Again All Over the World"

"Coming In On a Wing and a Prayer"

"Boogie Woogie Bugle Boy" – Andrews Sisters

"Don't Want to Walk Without You" – Harry James (a famous trumpeter)

"Waitin' for the Train to Come In" – Peggy Lee (our third or fourth cousin)

The era was one of romantic escape. Couples hurried into marriages in a few days' time – before the soldier or sailor was shipped out or while on furlough. He married the girl back home or someone of short acquaintance.

Movies told simple stories of folks back home or were patriotic war films with happy or heartbreaking endings. Not everyone made it back home but the sacrifice was worth it. John Wayne got off his horse to don a uniform. Others also took leave from acting to serve our country. "Destination Tokyo", "Best Years of Our Lives", "Anchors Away" and many other excellent films were made.

CHAPTER EIGHT

My favorite outing was boarding a Princess ship to Victoria, Canada for a day. These ships traveled back and forth with an affordable fare. Victoria was like something from a movie scene: hanging plants on light poles, the greenish copper on the top of their capital building, ships docking and leaving, ferry boats going between the islands, the Grand Empress Hotel with 188 rooms and their tea room with living plants in a glass enclosed room containing a pool, Beacon Park with horse-drawn "carriages" that drove through it and past the swans on the lake, and whistling servicemen in Canadian uniforms. These were the images I remember of Victoria. With trees and flowers, it was all so beautiful that I never tired of seeing it. We girls would go to the meat market to "ooh" and "ahh," almost drooling over the sight of all the meat.

The butcher asked us, "Can I help you?"

"No, thank you. We're just looking."

I wondered what he thought, but the meat was scarce in the US.

There were two trips that hold special memories for me. Aunt Irene was working in Wisconsin at an ammunition factory making parts for bombs. Toward the end of the war, she wanted to come to Seattle for work. She became my roommate. On a Princess overnight trip, she arose before I did and started her morning routine. I woke up when my head hit the bulkhead as we were going through wind and very high waves. She was walking toward me with toothpaste from one ear to the other. Usually she was easily frightened. This time she was staggering around to keep her balance and laughing at her dilemma. She had not experienced anything like this in South Dakota. These were special times with her as we were raised together and squabbled often as she was just five years older.

The other outing could be a story for a "two ships in the night" theme. It had a good plot, mystery ending and a handsome leading man.

Betty, one of the girls from our frat house and I spent a day in Victoria. On the return trip, we were below deck with other passengers gathered around a piano. We were singing songs of the era. "When the Light Goes On Again All Over the World" was a favorite that night. During blackouts people needed to pull dark shades or drapes over all their windows in a room when a light was on. Volunteers from neighborhoods were on duty to check for violations. Even lighting a cigarette outside was forbidden as any light that could be seen from the air could be dangerous. But these blackouts were only temporary, and as the war was ending, they were becoming less frequent.

"I'm going up on deck," I informed Betty.

"Why?"

"To see the lights as we approach Seattle. You can stay here and we'll get together later."

"OK."

I left the group, went up on deck to enjoy the quiet of the ship gliding effortlessly through the water. The steady rhythm of the motor, blending with the drifting music from below was so soothing. I had never dreamed of being on a sailing vessel, let alone enjoying it.

There was a slight breeze created by the movement of the ship. The evening was dark, making the sparkling trail of phosphorus visible in the water. The deck was deserted as I leaned on the rail to enjoy it. How peaceful after a day of activities!

Soon I sensed another presence not far from me. A naval officer came slowly out of the shadows and placed his arms on the rail. I could not make out his features but the white hat of a dress uniform gave me the clue that he was a naval officer. We gazed down into the water in silence.

"Why aren't you down below with the others?" He started the conversation.

"I like the quiet and never tire of seeing the lights of Seattle come into view," I replied.

There was more "small talk" until he observed, "There are the Seattle lights. Our journey is almost over."

The announcements came loud and clear over the speaker, "We are docking shortly. Check for all your belongings and be prepared to disembark. Please go immediately to pick up your baggage."

We stood there to watch the docking, said our farewells and then left in different directions. The piano below was silent, replaced by footsteps scurrying about. Betty came up and off we went.

There were no baggage carousels – just bags dumped in a special area. We were walking by the baggage pile when I heard, "We meet again". There stood the officer whose name and rank are no longer in my memory. I shall refer to him as "Officer." Betty and I wanted to get home so it was annoying to stop for a chat.

"Are you hungry?"

The magic words! Of course I was hungry as it was after 6 p.m.

"I would like you to have dinner with me."

Betty had wandered off so I informed him that we were together. He picked up his bag, saw Betty returning and asked, "Are you hungry? Would you like to join us for dinner?" She quickly sized up the situation – a free dinner plus being with an officer. She knew he would take us to a nice place and she was hungry too. Besides, we were to help our servicemen! She glanced at me and then agreed. Now he had two Boeing girls.

He was a polite, well-mannered and pleasant dinner companion. We did eat in a nice restaurant with oversized menus.

When the waiter came to the table, the officer ordered for all three of us. That was a first! Betty and I glanced at each other wondering about that.

"Do you like what I ordered?"

"Oh yes, yes. Fine."

Everything was delicious. He asked me if he could take me out again as we were going to the bus stop. He had been refreshingly polite and a gentleman, so I gave him my phone number and address. During the war the servicemen were on the move thus no time for a relationship. He was calm and mature; it was a delightful change.

The next dinner date was similar but different. We went in a taxi to one of the best seafood places in Seattle. He ordered us baked oysters! What was I going to do? I had eaten small oysters in stew but I downed them with crackers. Maybe the larger baked ones would be different. When the waiter put the dish before me they looked delicious. The aroma was pleasing to the nostrils but the first bite.... I managed to swallow it with other food. He noticed my skirting around the oyster dish.

"Don't you like baked oysters?" he asked.

"I've never had them before. At home we had stew with the small ones."

He immediately called the waiter, told him to take it away and bring me a fish that I liked.

"Oh, no! It's OK as I have plenty of other food."

He turned a deaf ear being very gracious and matter-of-fact about it. He went on as if nothing had happened.

When he paid the check, I walked over to the right of the cashier as I had been told that it was not polite to hover while a man paid. There was a glass case nearby so I looked into it. There was an unusual necklace made of polished clam shells held together with white ring-like chain links. The shells were of different colored pastels, smooth and satiny. The necklace fascinated me so much that I didn't see the officer coming toward me.

"Find something you like?"

"I'm fascinated by how those shells in that necklace could be so smooth with such delicate pastel colors. It is so beautiful."

He called to the person at the cash register. "We would like a necklace from here, please."

"Oh, no!" I protested. "I was just admiring it."

"You like it, don't you?"

"Yes, but...."

He was already paying for it. I was sick with embarrassment. It seemed as if every eye was on me. Never take a gift from a man, Grandma had warned me, so I knew about "kept women". I started for the door.

"Just a minute. Turn around and I'll put this on for you."

"Thanks," I said weakly as I lifted up my hair.

How good it was to be outside and revived by the fresh Seattle air. I felt more "cleansed" somehow.

The ride home in the taxi was endless but a treat. Waiting for a bus and riding in one was the norm. He was gracious as ever, seeming to think all was OK. I thanked him for the dinner and the necklace as soon as I saw the frat house. He did not ask for another dinner date as he was leaving soon. I was relieved to shut the door behind me. It wasn't long before I got over the guilt and enjoyed the necklace. People admired it for many years to come.

The phone rang a couple of nights later. It was the officer.

"I'm going out of town for about a week. I've made plans to go pheasant hunting in South Dakota."

"South Dakota!" I broke in. "That's my state!"

We used to eat so many pheasants in the fall that I thought I never wanted to see another one. But now my mouth watered.

"Where are you hunting?"

"Around Huron."

"I can't believe my ears! My great aunt and uncle live in Huron. I can give you their address and phone number. If you need anything, give them a call. They would be happy to help you."

"Thanks."

I gave him the information, we talked a bit and then he hung up.

The next phone call stated, "Hello, Roverta?"

"Aunt Sarah?...Oh, Aunt Sarah! She always pronounced my name wrong.

The surprise shook me and homesickness returned like a flood. How I longed to see her!

"Are you ill? Are you all right? Is something the matter?"

Regaining some composure and wiping away the tears, I replied, "Oh, no. I'm all right. It is so good to hear from you."

"Your nice gentleman friend said we could talk as long as we wanted."

No one from home had called so this was such a treat.

"Here's your Uncle Pat." She finally gave him his turn.

He was a man of few words but did well, probably relieved that everything was going well. It was he who had urged me to go to Seattle.

"Your friend wants to talk to you so I won't say too much more. That was so nice of him to do this."

Tears filled my eyes as we said our goodbyes. The officer had forewarned me to be sure to watch for the mail every day as he was sending some pheasants that would need cooking right away.

"Thank you for the call, I replied. It was so good to talk to my aunt and uncle. I miss them."

He repeated the order to watch for the package.

"I will. What a treat they will be and thank you again so much." We hung up and that was the last I ever heard from him.

The pheasants, packed in dry ice arrived safely. They were so tasty, but there was no way to let him know. Many questions were left unanswered. Where was he? Who was he? Did he have a family? Did he make it home after the war? Where was his home?

CHAPTER NINE

Toward the end of the war an extraordinary experience softened my heart toward uniformed men and the whole conflict. In the evenings when the girls had no dates and personal chores were finished, we'd go out somewhere together. Adeline and two other girls had a free night so I was asked if I would like to join them in going to the Crystal Ballroom. The change of pace appealed to me. The Crystal was more tranquil with regular dances – no jitter bugging. It just had *Cha Cha Cha* and the like.

"Sounds like a plan," I anxiously replied.

Off we went to the bus stop. It was a nice evening with no rain or drizzle. The reliable transportation stopped close to the ballroom.

"Here we go, gals. I wonder if that man who teaches will be here tonight? I'd like to learn that last folk dance better."

We checked our wraps and surveyed the dancers. There was the same mixture of armed forces, more subdued but enjoying themselves. The gentleman with gray hair was there to teach the folk dances which were interspersed during the evening.

After dancing a few times, Adeline asked, "Who do you have the next dance with?"

Before I could answer, there was a slight commotion at the door. We stood mesmerized as a Canadian army sergeant and two privates from Canada entered. The lady chaperon walked over. There was laughing as the men came in. She was not amused yet did not look as stern as usual.

"It only happens in the movies," "Across a crowded room," "Two ships that meet in the night". All these sayings plus instant attraction from afar does not occur often in real life, but this was a "magical ballroom".

"With him," I heard myself saying as I gazed at a handsome man at the door.

"What?"

"I've got the next dance with him."

She followed my gaze toward the Sergeant.

"Oh, sure. You and me both!"

The pleasant notes of the waltz drifted over the ballroom. Dancers, including Adeline and her partner, began to glide around the room. I wandered over to the band just listening to the melody.

"Wanna dance?" a sailor asked.

"No, thanks." Now why did I say that? I was a USO hostess trained to never turn down a serviceman.

"How about this dance?" a soldier invited.

"No, thanks." I couldn't believe my ears seeing as I disliked being a wallflower. Fortunately, there were plenty of girls there that night. I stared at the band half listening when there was a tap on my shoulder.

"How about this dance?"

I nodded "yes" even before I turned around. I knew it was him.

We stood for a moment in eye contact and then drifted in with the other dancers. No words were spoken. It was like "two peas in a pod", "salt and pepper", "cream and sugar" all rolled into one. We were in step the entire time with a little light talk. He was a good height for me, like Harland. He held me in the proper dancing position. I felt relaxed not having to comprehend his next move.

Adeline spotted us. Her eyes opened wide and her jaw dropped in astonishment. Every time her partner would swing her around, her head would snap back to look in disbelief. The music stopped and Marty escorted me to the sidelines. We had exchanged names so he thanked me by name and walked away. Adeline came in like a rushing wind.

"How did you do that? How did you know he'd be your next partner?"

I smiled, shrugged my shoulders and floated away in my dream world. It was a mystery to me also. The crystal ball hanging from the ceiling rotated slowly around – reflecting and casting its spell like a wand scattering stars.

Marty was talking to everyone he passed leaving smiles behind. Now I know the word – charisma. He was pretending to have a dog on a leash, showing people and telling them about it. Amazingly, many reached down to pet the imaginary pet.

When the music resumed, he asked me to be his partner again. As we danced by the chaperon, he stopped a moment to ask her to hold the leash until he returned. My heart sank. But then she took the leash. A half smile curled her lips into a full one. I had never seen that. We returned for the invisible dog when that dance was over. She handed him the unseen leash and he thanked her.

During the final dance he asked to see me home. We girls had a rule that if plans changed, it was all right. I told them to go without me. Adeline had already left at eleven for her shift. It was irresistible not to prolong the evening as it had been so enjoyable. He asked for my coat check, called the privates to stay with me until he returned from the hatcheck.

A sailor came up to me and asked, "Do you have a match?" The privates moved in before I could reply.

"No, she doesn't. Move on." He hesitated then decided it wasn't worth the hassle to protest. Two to one wasn't a good ratio.

Marty returned, held my coat, and gently pulled it up over my shoulders. The four of us descended the stairs after a goodbye to our chaperone.

"You guys can do whatever you want to. See you at the base." He dismissed them as we reached the street. We headed for the bus stop.

As we passed the movie theater, he asked, "Shall we take in a movie?"

"Why not?" I agreed.

The lateness of the hour never entered my mind. Boeing and early rising seemed far away.

Just being together, holding hands or having his arm around me made me feel cozy and comfy. His hand was protecting, a security I missed. Servicemen attended these all-night movies to spend as much time as possible off the base or ship. Plus, it saved on hotel room rates. The YMCA was affordable but filled up early. We found the theater to be a place where we could be together just a little longer.

We sat through a double feature. Leaving the building, we watched the dawn breaking over the city. It brought us to our senses.

"I will be AWOL (absent without leave), but I will find a taxi and get you back home," Marty stated.

"No, you get going. I'll take the 60 or 710 bus – whichever comes first."

Living near the university district gave me a choice of two lines.

"No, I want to see that you get home safely," he replied.

"I'll be all right," I assured him.

He left after a few more insistences that it was important he not be AWOL. I watched as he ran looking back, concern clouding the perpetual smile.

Seattle was strangely silent at dawn. The streets were practically deserted. I looked at my watch. The busses did not start their runs for another 20 minutes. I felt so alone and insecure after all of Marty's protection. Weariness enveloped my body as I stood waiting. What had I done staying out all night? How could I get through the workday? Would I get home in time to change and be ready for my ride?

A bit of calmness returned as I settled in the bus seat. Wonder what the bus driver thought of my standing on the corner at dawn? Then there would be the girls' questions to face. Would Marty make it back to the base on time? There was too much to handle that early in the morning.

Due to the fewer stops to pick up passengers, there was time for a bubble bath. No problem being first in line this morning. The warm froth soothed away the fatigue that had crept over my whole being.

"Who's in there?"

"Me," I said, startled out of a doze. "I'll be out in a minute."

The questions came as the girls arose yawning. Most of them were concerned for my well-being. The two who had met Marty buzzed about his humor and charm. Somehow I made it to the carpool on time, stayed awake – sort of – during the day and had a short nap before dinner. Marty had requested my phone number to call and be assured that I had made it home safely. His call came that evening. He was not AWOL. He informed me of his next leave and asked if we could get together. You know my answer.

Numerous leaves were spent in delightful activities with the gang at the frat house. They looked forward to his coming. Alta took a shine to him, always pleased to see him. "Platter parties" were popular with all of us. Someone would buy the latest 78 record of a big band or famous vocalist. We would listen, sing along or talk. This may seem dull to some, but it was quite the opposite. Marty and "Sherlock Holmes" (Arthur) kept things lively. All of us had experiences to share with ample enthusiasm because this present life was new to all of us. We blocked out tomorrow.

I yearned to attend college, but the nearest I came was living near one in the frat house. Marty came one Sunday afternoon. It happened to be a gorgeous fall day, so we chose to walk to the university. Trees with huge amber leaves lined the street leading into the main entrance. We walked hand in hand under the archway of color. Occasionally, a leaf lazily floated down onto our path.

We entered onto a rich green lawn that wrapped itself around a reflection pool. We sat on the cement rim of the pool, absorbing the quiet beauty all around. Walks snaked their way to or around the buildings. Now and then a female student wearing a sweater, skirt and saddle shoes would walk by. A boy attired in a sweater, sporting football or rowing team letter, long pants and saddle shoes would stroll by. A few others dotted the area, some perched under a tree or stretched out on the grass. Their eyes were focused on the large book they were holding. Probably an exam was scheduled on Monday. I loved to pretend I was a college student. The tranquility of the campus was heavenly.

White clouds drifting in flawless blue reflected in the pool. Marty reached his finger in the water, disturbing that picture. I do not recall our conversation. The six o'clock campus chimes filled the air with music. Sunset was approaching, so we resumed our walk going in the direction of Alta's frat house. Something would be happening there or we would go to dinner.

Once, one of the Coast Guard presented Alta with some Hershey candy bars. The servicemen had access to items like that. (Any guy could get a date with chocolate or a pair of nylon stockings.) Alta pooled our sugar coupons, obtained butter some way and used the chocolate to make a batch of fudge for us. Those present were more than surprised. "Oohs" and "ahhs", licking of lips, hugs for Alta and savoring each bite showed our deep appreciation.

We spent Marty's last night at such a gathering. He was showered with goodbyes and good luck from everyone before they retreated to the sofas or out of the door. A few lamps dimly lit the room.

Marty looked at me and said, "I want you to listen to something before I go." I followed him to the phonograph. He wound the machine, put a record on the turntable, started it and carefully lowered the needle arm onto the outer rim of the record.

A soft melody came forth before the words began:

> *"All of a sudden my heart sings,*
> *When I remember the little things.*
> *The way you dance and hold me tight.*
> *The way you kiss and say goodnight.*
> *The crazy things we say and do.*
> *The fun it is to be with you.*
> *The magic thrill that's in your touch.*
> *Oh, darling, I love you so much."*

I stared at the record going round and round. My anger was almost uncontrollable when I realized he had broken down my wall of hatred and defense that I had built up because of Harland. I did not want to care about anyone again but just wished to say "goodbye," forget, and go on to the next day. I placed my hand on the phonograph to keep from stopping the record. I did not want anyone to care for me and then go off to fight.

> *"The secret way you press my hand,*
> *To let me know you understand.*
> *The wind and rain upon your face,*
> *The breathless world of your embrace.*
> *Your little laugh and half surprise*
> *The starlight gleaming in your eyes.*

Remembering all those little things,
All of a sudden my heart sings."

I relaxed, remembering the good times we had.

"All of a sudden my heart sings,
When I remember little things,
Your voice on the telephone,
That crazy laugh that's all your own,
The way you smile lights up your eyes.
The way you look up in surprise,
The magic thrill that's in your touch,
Oh, darling, I love you so much."

All of a Sudden My Heart Sings.
© Warner/Chappell Music, Inc., Universal Music
Publishing Group. Songwriters: Harold Rome,
Janblan, and Laurent Herpin

He put his hand on mine and said, "This is how I feel."

I did not look at him or comment. For once I was speechless. He removed the record, placed it in the wrapper and handed it to me.

"I want you to have this."

"Thanks."

"If I write to you, will you answer?"

I nodded my head "yes" and walked him to the door. After our goodbyes, he walked away, not looking back.

"That's that," I thought. "Now back to the ol' routine."

In a few days I found a letter in the mail. It was brief and simple, yet the picture he drew at the bottom of the page said more than words could say. A perfectly shaped duck in bold pencil was drawn walking across the bottom of the page from the left side all the way to the right. Teardrops fell from the duck's eyes all the way back to the left side of the page.

"I miss you."

I shed a few "duck tears," too upon finishing the letter. There were other letters, some with pictures, but none to top that first one.

Alta and the girls were anxious for the arrival of his communications, part of which I shared. It was good to be really living again but always in the background were the deaths of so many plus the unbelievable destruction that was still occurring in our nation. We were unaware of living in the era that would change our way of life and go down in history as THE WAR.

One day Alta met me at the door when I came home from my shift. She looked grim and handed me a letter. I saw my handwriting plus a large "No return address" stamped in red on the letter. I checked to see if the address was correct and was puzzled. She told me that Marty had died. I knew she was wrong and took the letter upstairs to my room. Every other possibility seemed to fade as I stared at those red words. So what? Just another one fallen, but my heart was telling me that was not so.

Everyone was talking about their day and evening plans when we sat around the dinner table that night. My silence was too much for Alta. She informed the girls of my returned letter. It was as if a bomb had been dropped on my life. They sat in unbelief. Marty was so full of life. It was difficult to think he had been taken from this world. They finished dinner, attempted to console me and then disappeared to their rooms. I wasn't quite ready to face them so I stayed downstairs.

"Would you like for me to take the letter to the Red Cross to see if they can find out how it happened?" Alta asked.

"Yes. Thanks. I'll go get it."

About a couple of days later she learned that he had been killed in a truck accident on the base. Where is the good in all of this? The answers came slowly as time went on. He loved people and life. He had enjoyed his time with us. He wasn't sent to the front nor did he ever have to kill anyone. The war was accelerating for a major attack. The casualties would probably number in the thousands. He escaped that and the possibility of ever being tortured in an enemy camp or prison. As time passed, I chose to accept this horrific news rather than continuing to mourn his loss. Marty would have wanted me to continue living a life as he so loved it. I was at peace. All of us benefited from Alta's effort and went on to do our part for victory.

Life does go on. One day I looked at Marty's address on the red-lettered envelope one last time and threw the envelope away.

"Sgt. C.S. Martineau." What did the C and S stand for? He was just Marty. "67th Ord. Co. A, Canada." The reason I am including his story, which I have never told before, is that he had such a positive influence on my life. He changed my outlook on disappointments for which I am grateful.

CHAPTER TEN

Ernie Pyle was an American journalist who was known as a roving correspondent. He desired to live with different infantry units on or near the front lines to report the truth about these men. He was allowed to do so, resulting in his columns reflecting the perspective of the common soldier that won him popularity and acclaim. In one column he wrote, "Their life consisted wholly and solely of war, for they were and always had been front line Infantry men. They survived because the fates were kind to them, certainly — but, also, because they had become hard and immensely wise in animal-like ways of self-preservation."

He reported from the United States, Europe, Africa and the Pacific. He was nearly killed by the bombing in Normandy. Pyle came home to recuperate but wanted to go to the Pacific because his heart was still with the infantry. He was allowed to go to the invasion of Okinawa. In 1945 Pyle died on an island off Okinawa. He was the target of a Japanese sniper. His legacy contains many honors including the Purple Heart, one of the highest military honors given in the United States for heroic acts above and beyond the call of duty.

A film, "The Story of G. I. Joe", was produced as a tribute to the infantry. The dialogue was taken from Pyle's columns. The movie's premier was held two months after he was killed in action.

Periodically, President Roosevelt sent information over the radio to bolster us up. His famous quote after the attack on Pearl Harbor was, "Remember Pearl Harbor." General Wainwright and other military leaders gave assurance that we would win if everyone "buckled down." Winston Churchill in England remarked, "We've just begun to fight."

President Roosevelt died before the victory was won. Vice President Harry Truman assumed the duties of the office. Tremendous pressure was put on him. The United States had the atomic bomb that would totally destroy an area but leave radiation behind. The land would be barren. The decision was made to warn the Japanese that bombs would be dropped on their country if they did not surrender. This decision was made to end or to shorten the war and save the lives of the Allies. Japan refused to surrender.

People here in America were fearful of the mass destruction. So many innocent people would lose their lives. On August 6, 1945 the first atomic bomb named "Little Boy" exploded over Hiroshima, Japan. About 75,000 people died instantly; another 70,000 were injured. Thousands died from burns and radiation. The results were more horrible than imagined. The ones who survived were badly burned. Some suffered from radiation for years afterward.

A beautiful Boeing B-29 – the Enola Gay – carried that first powerful bomb. Men wore special glasses so they would not be blinded by the intense flash. The cloud of smoke formed a giant mushroom miles high in the sky. It was more frightening than anticipated.

Newspaper article depicting Japan's Emperor Hirohito and a sample of an atomic bomb mushroom cloud.

The Japanese refused to surrender. A second bomb, "Fat Man" was dropped on Nagasaki August 9, 1945. An estimated 50,000 were killed instantly. The Imperial Council voted 3-3 on surrender. Emperor Hirohito came forward to break the tie. The terms of surrender were debated within the Japanese government. President Truman had no response by the 13th so ordered the firebomb air raids to continue. Thousands more Japanese lost their lives while their leaders delayed. August 15th the Emperor announced the surrender.

Details had to be worked out, but finally on September 2 a formal surrender ceremony took place on the deck of the USS Missouri an-chored in Tokyo Bay.

(Sources: Associated Press, Wikipedia, CIA)

Years later people still questioned Truman's wisdom in using this drastic means – the atomic bombs. My opinion: Sad as it was for the Japanese, we needed to do it. We wanted our troops to come home. The Japanese people were at the mercy of their leaders. Their men would rather die than "lose face." Suicide bombers hit ships and other targets. Surrender was not an option in that culture.

The signing of the peace treaty was quite an historical event except it was not the end but the beginning of "mop up." Countries were assisted in rebuilding the damage caused by the conflict.

"Lights came on again all over the world." People flooded the streets when hearing the victory announcements. We gals went into downtown Seattle that night. It was like New Year's Eve in Times Square or crowds gathered to get a glimpse of the queen or a department store sale all rolled into one. People, young and old, were jumping up and down, ringing bells, tooting horns and hugging whomever. A sailor came toward us. He was kissing girls on the cheek. We received a victory kiss. The glee was intoxicating. We began to join in.

The tone changed at Boeing the following week. Mr. Whitmore handed me a stack of termination papers.

"We are beginning to discharge people. Production is returning to normal so we will not need all these workers. You can start figuring their wages and type that and other information on these papers. Here is a list of names."

This was interspersed with tearful hugs, "So long" and "Been good to know you." Groups were brought to the hanger area for pictures. They punched the time clock for the last time and handed in their ID buttons. Mr. Whitmore requested I remain as his secretary. I was thankful.

Alta had to give up the frat house. It was like breaking up a family. Adeline, who was dating Alta's son, Bill, went back to North Dakota and married her boyfriend from high school. We kept in touch until the day she died. Sherlock married Dimples, one of the Boeing girls, and became a minister in Canada. Juanita and her sister returned to Minnesota. Everyone scattered into his or her next phase of life. Alta wrote to me through the years plus I visited her twice after I left the state.

A couple had advertised rooms for rent to young ladies. The family lived on the main floor and rented the upstairs bedrooms. A cozy living room, kitchen and laundry room were available for the renters. The location was close and in the university district. Ideal! They accepted me. It was here that Aunt Irene joined me. We had an east room with a balcony. On Sundays I could sit out there and hear the campus chimes – when it wasn't raining, of course.

Bill was very lonesome after Adeline left. He was in shock really. We took in a baseball game now and then. I enjoyed going over to their house to talk or have some dinner as I was lonesome, too. Alta, her other son, Gene, and her sister were usually present.

Alta planned a clam dig insisting I go along. What an experience! She and Bill packed up a tent, sleeping bags, quilts, shovels, containers for the clams that did not escape the shovels and whatever else that was needed. We left early in the evening to allow time to set up camp and retire early. That was fine with me.

Putting up the tent and Alta making our "sleeping nests" was a scene to watch. A large piece of oilcloth, usually used for tablecloths, was put on the ground first. She said this was to keep the moisture from the ground coming up into our bedding. Next she added the padding of quilts on which were placed the sleeping bags and pillows. The tent was pitched near the beach. It was beginning to get cool and damp. Those "nests" looked inviting and were soon occupied.

"Time to get up! Everybody up! Get your shovel and pail. Let's go!!" Alta startled me awake.

"What time is it?" I groaned.

"Time to get digging."

It was four or five o'clock in the morning! My nose was cold so I put my head down into the sleeping bag. Crawling out of that warm cocoon was pure torture with more to come. A scarf tied on my head and a jacket over my clothing helped restore some heat. But stepping out on that ice-cold sand in bare feet sent a chill all the way through my body. Alta said bare feet were necessary. She was right as we had to walk along the water's edge with frigid waves splashing over our feet. We watched for little bubbling holes in the sand as the ocean receded. They indicated where the clams lived and we dug, bringing them up from their sandy homes. It became fun after my legs became numb up to my knees. Results: delicious clam chowder, another dish I learned to like. However, that was my one and only clam dig.

Mr. Whitmore approached me one morning with a more serious look than usual.

"I'm sorry, but you will have to be terminated. I tried to keep you on, but the union insisted that you have to go. I will type your termination paper for you if you like."

"No, thanks. I'll do it."

I soon came to realize he had not done me a favor by keeping me there. Jobs had been gobbled up by those laid off before me. Another problem was that I looked too young to have had the experience listed on my resume. I did not qualify when shorthand was required. There had not been an opportunity to continue my post-grad work after I left to take care of Gram, Aunt Ceil and family in Rapid City, South Dakota.

The Mason Clinic had an opening for which I qualified. There were approximately ten or twelve typists at desks lined up in a row. They typed doctors' reports from their files and any other information that was requested. I joined their ranks. It turned out to be like a classroom as the lady boss sat in a room that had a large glass window from which she could watch our every move. If we talked to anyone near us, she reprimanded us loudly and told us to keep our minds on our work. We agonized under her iron rule. I was spared by being transferred to the counter where the clinic dispensed insulin to diabetics.

CHAPTER ELEVEN

The next and last job I had in Seattle was at Buda Engine Company. The manager took a chance and hired me. He, too, asked me if I took shorthand but I said "No". They had a teletype machine which was used most of the time. I did not know what that was. I told him that I had never used one but was willing to learn so he gave me the opportunity. (Aunt Sarah had given me the advice that you can learn, so speak up when getting a job.) He told me to start the following Monday morning.

The office was an open area near the front door with the window facing the street. It was a pleasant, sunny spot with activity all around. It opened into a showroom of various sized engines. Some were huge.

The teletype was fun and amazing to me. How could a machine answer me? There it was clicking back words on a screen. A few times the words did not reflect business.

The job did not last too long. The boss hired another girl who soon began to have lunch with him, a married man. The shop men showed their dislike of her with looks and unkind words behind her back. (Later, I heard that the loudest complainer divorced his wife and married her.) A higher-up came by to check out the business and told my boss that this was a one-girl office. The boss fired me using the reason that I did not take shorthand, even though it wasn't necessary. I even had seniority.

My diary stated, "December 11, 1946. Left for Los Angeles."

"War buddies" Linda and Charlene had gone there immediately after the war ended. I had contacted Den who had been honorably discharged from the Navy and working at his former job in Los Angeles. He had met the gals and helped them get around to see places of interest. They wrote glowing reports and begged me to join them. I closed that chapter of my life in Seattle and started a new one in California.

Patriotism, determination, courage, cooperation and, above all, God's grace brought us through WWII. The loss of lives and money was enormous. Wounded soldiers filled veterans' homes. Families missing loved ones "picked up the pieces" and continued life without them. Freedom is not free.

The war years were not the "good ol' days" that grandmas like to talk about, but ones of learning about and experiencing a different time and place. It was to make a better world for you, dear granddaughter.

CPSIA information can be obtained at www.ICGtesting.com
Printed in the USA
LVOW100945150312

273209LV00002B/5/P